丘の四季

前田真三写真集

丘の四季
HILLS OF COLOR
Scenes and Seasons

Photographed by
SHINZO MAEDA

Design & Layout by Go Asanuma+ G&A Studio
Translated by Ernest & Matsue Richter

丘

「丘」という言葉には、明るく軽やかなイメージがある。そしてそこには、ロマンの響きさえ感じられる。しかし残念ながらわが国には、その語感にふさわしいような風景はほとんどないといってもよい。ただし、北海道中央部の旭川市から富良野市に至る間の丘陵地帯には、まさしく「丘」と呼ぶにふさわしいおおらかな景観が広がっている。

この付近一帯の丘は、人工的に整地された畑作地帯であるからやや野趣に欠ける面もあるが、ジャガイモをはじめ小麦やビートなど西洋的な作物が多く、ゆるやかな丘の連なりはヨーロッパの田園に匹敵する洒落た風景であるといっても決して過言ではないであろう。

私は、過去二度にわたり通算四ヶ月間英国各地を取材して歩いたことがある。イングランドの田園地帯を車で走っていた時、ふと北海道の丘と錯覚したこともあった。それ程この丘がイギリスの田園風景とよく似ているということであろう。

英国の場合、わが国と違って国土全体が同じような田園風景の連続であるからスケールも大きいし、農家や牧舎なども古い歴史を感じさせる風格のある建物が多く、どこにカメラを向けても絵になる風景が果てしなく続いている。広がりや建造物の面では英国の田園風景に及ばないものの、北海道のこの丘は、大雪山をはじめたえず噴煙を空に巻き上げている十勝岳や芦別岳等の山々に囲まれていて、その立体的な景観は、英国のそれよりある面でははるかに勝っているように思える。

初めてこの丘の一角に立って、五体が痺れる程の感激を味わったのがつい昨日のように思えるが、それから既に十数年の歳月が流れている。その間数限りなく訪ねているが、いつ訪れても丘はその時々に違った表情を見せてくれる。永い間には、再び巡り合うことのできないであろうドラマチックな光景に幾度か出合って来た。何度訪れても飽きることがなく、通えば通う程にその良さが判って来て、この丘への思いは更に募るばかりである。

その後時代の変遷と共にこの丘の様相もかなり変わってきた。かつては一人の観光客もいなかったこの丘に、年を追って訪れる人も急増している。そして以前にも増して早い速度で丘の形態そのものも変わりつつある。私の写真は、記録を目的に撮影したものではないが、既にこの丘から失われてしまった風景もたくさんある。そうした意味から、今回、十数年来の丘の表情を過去に発表した写真も交えて、ここに改めて『丘の四季』と題する一冊の写真集に編集したものである。

前田真三

Foreword

Shinzo Maeda

The word "hill" summons up feelings that are bright, airy, one might almost say literary. However, I am afraid those adjectives apply to very few places in Japan. The only exception that comes to mind is the setting of these photographs, the hilly country of central Hokkaido between Asahikawa and Furano. There one can find the broad, scenic beauty of true hills.

The hills in that area have been cultivated, and so the scenery is not that of untouched nature. Most of the crops are western types —— potatoes, wheat, beets and the like, and indeed it would not be an exaggeration to say that those gently rolling slopes are as charming as the rural vistas of Europe.

I have been to England twice, spending a total of four months travelling and taking photos, and the landscape in that country is so similar to that of the hill country of Hokkaido that sometimes while driving through the English countryside, I had the feeling that I was back among the hills of Hokkaido. But the English scenery differs from that of Hokkaido; in the former there is a sameness that imparts breadth, that widens the scale of things. Then, too, there are many old buildings——farmhouses and barns redolent with historical atmosphere. This picturesque scenery can be photographed from any angle and excels Hokkaido in its expanse and the presence of the old buildings. But the hills of Hokkaido, surrounded by the swirling volcanic smoke of Mt. Daisetsu and the other nearby peaks, has a three-dimensional beauty that is superior in its own way.

It has been fifteen or sixteen years since my first stroll upon the hills of Hokkaido, but it seems like only yesterday. That first meeting with the hills impressed me so deeply that I felt as if my whole body had gone numb. Since then I have made countless revisits, but the hills always show me different faces, and over the years there have been many occasions when I have experienced moments of dramatic beauty that I know will never again occur. I won't tire of those hills; the more I visit them, the more attractive I find them. My feelings for the hills of Hokkaido are now the feelings of love.

The appearance of the hills has considerably changed with the passing of time. In the old days, the area had no sightseers, but now their numbers are increasing every year. Moreover, the actual contours of the hills are changing much more rapidly than before, and though my photographs are never taken for the purpose of keeping records, I find in them graphic evidence of the disappearance of much of the old scenery. It is to preserve the memory of the hills I love that I have compiled this collection of photographs, "Hills of Color——Scenes and Seasons."

HILLS OF COLOR Scenes and Seasons — 丘の四季

春 春の遅い北国では、四月に入ってようやく雪が消え、待ちかねたかのように一斉に農作業が始まる。丘は入念に耕され、美しい畝が大地に刻まれる。雪の下で冬をしのいで来た秋蒔き麦や牧草も生気を取り戻す。本格的な春の到来は、木々が芽吹き、エゾヤマザクラのピンクの花やスモモ、梨などの白い花が丘のあちこちに目立つようになる四月下旬から五月にかけてである。

夏 夏、木々の緑が日毎に濃さを増し、作物も順調に成長を続ける。初夏の晴れた日には、大雪、十勝の青い山並に残雪が眩しい。七月から八月にかけては、この丘が最も豊かな彩りを見せる時期である。緑から黄そして褐色へと稔って行く麦畑、ジャガイモや大根の白い花、紫色のラベンダーなど、どれをとっても雄大で色彩鮮やかな光景が展開される。

秋 秋は穫り入れの季節である。九月になると朝晩は、めっきり冷え込むようになる。澄みきった青空のもとで、穫り入れに余念のない人々には、収穫の喜びが満ち溢れている。やがて木々が色づき始める頃、高山から低山そして丘へと新雪が訪れる。その雪の訪れにせきたてられるように人々は、収穫に精を出す。

冬 冬の丘は、白い世界である。早い年には、十月中旬に訪れた初雪はやがて断続的に降り続け、十二月になると根雪になる。春から秋へと様々な色彩に彩られて来た丘も、白一色の雪景色となる。一月、二月と冷え込む時には、零下30度以下に下がることもある。冴えわたった寒気のもとに広がる雪の丘は悲しいまでに美しく、幻想的ですらある。そして三月、まだ一面の雪景色の中でようやくフキノトウが顔をのぞかせる頃、人々は融雪剤を撒く。一日でも早く丘に春が訪れることを待ち望んで――。

Spring comes rather late in the northernmost regions of Japan; the snow does not finally disappear until early April, and only then do farmers start working after their long wait for the melting of the snow. The hills are plowed with extra care and now beautiful furrows appear on the surface of the earth, but true spring arrives only when the plants start budding and blooming at the end of April or the beginning of May.

Summer is a time of enrichment. With each passing day, the leaves become a deeper green and the crops a little closer to their ripening. July and August are the months when the hills reach a peak in color; golden-yellow wheat fields, white potato blossoms, lavender-covered hillocks —— all of these are capable of creating scenes of great natural splendour.

Autumn brings the harvest season, and farmers working toward the harvest labor spiritedly under clear blue skies. Later, when the leaves change color, the first snow appears on the high mountains, then on the lower slopes and finally atop the hills.

Winter arrives. In some years, the first snow falls in mid-October and continues intermittently, creating a snow cover that lasts till spring. The land which displayed the varied colors of spring and summer now becomes a world of white, and the snowy hills stretching out in the clear cold air sometimes possess an almost melancholy beauty.

朝霧の丘・美瑛町　Morning mist over the hills　5

　待ちわびた春・上富良野町　The long-awaited coming of spring

爛漫エゾヤマザクラ・美瑛町　Wild cherry trees in full bloom

緑風の丘・美瑛町　Green breezes cross the hills　*11*

桜咲く道・富良野市　Blossom-lined road

菜の花咲く牧場・美瑛町　Meadow bright with rape blossoms

白い花の咲く頃・美瑛町　A time for white blossoms

夕映の丘・美瑛町　Evening radiance

残雪十勝連峰・美瑛町　The last snows on the Tokachi Mountains　*17*

消毒をする人々・美瑛町　Preparing the soil

22　初夏のジャガイモ畑・美瑛町　Potato fields in early summer

麦秋多彩・美瑛町　Varicolored grain awaiting harvest

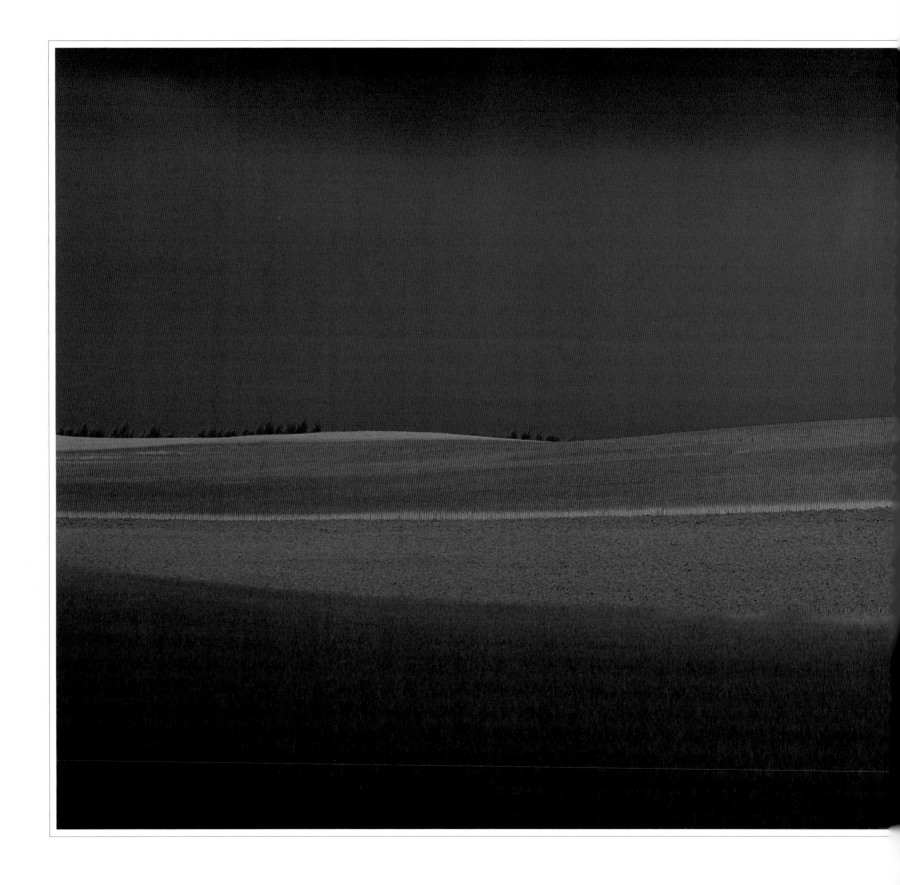

ポピー咲く深山峠・上富良野町　Poppy flowers at Miyama Pass

芳香ラベンダー・上富良野町　A sea of fragrant lavender

麦秋暮色・上富良野町　Graceful fields colored by the evening sky　*31*

　ジャガイモ咲く津郷農場・上富良野町　White potato blossoms

残光無限・美瑛町　Day lingers on

十勝岳盛夏・美瑛町　Mt. Tokachi in midsummer

夏雲の丘・上富良野町　Soaring summer clouds

日の出公園ラベンダー園・上富良野町　Hinodeyama lavender field

初秋の稲田・中富良野町　Early autumn rice paddies　*41*

朝霧の日輪・上富良野町　Sun-glazed morning mist

取り入れ間近・美瑛町　Just before the harvest

　路傍の秋草・美瑛町　Autumn wildflowers along a country road

原生林紅葉・美瑛町　The autumn colors of a virgin forest

秋の日差し・美瑛町　Autumn sunlight

56 | 残りもみじ・美瑛町 Late season maple

朝霧に浮かぶ十勝岳・美瑛町　Mt. Tokachi floating on the morning mist

夕月オプタテシケ山・美瑛町　Moon over Mt. Oputateshike

新雪淡く・美瑛町　The season's first light touch of snow

畝の彼方に・上富良野町　Green-edged furrows on a wheat field

新雪来たる・美瑛町　Approaching snow

晩秋の晴れ間・美瑛町　A clear moment in late autumn

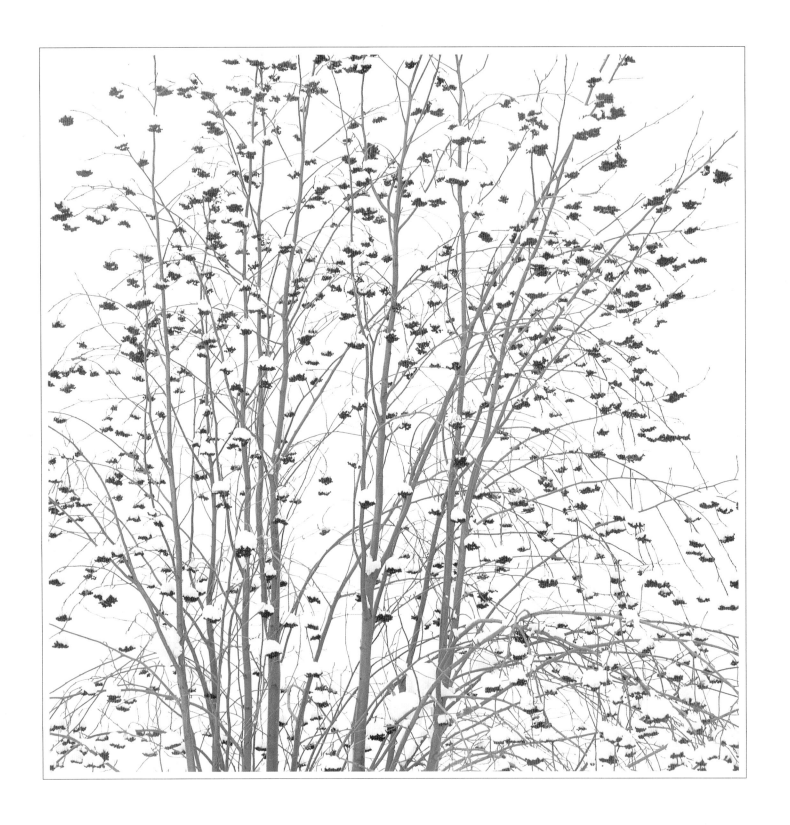

雪のナナカマド・美瑛町　Mountain ash tree in the snow

樹間の芦別岳・美瑛町　Mt. Ashibetsu seen through a curtain of trees

暮れゆく大雪山・美瑛町　Painted mountain sunset on Mt. Daisetsu　73

雪原の落葉松・上富良野町　Larch trees on a snow-blanketed field

夕映の落葉松林・美瑛町　Larch forest dyed with evening light

霧氷の深山峠・上富良野町　Silver branches at Miyama Pass | 77

きらめく丘・上富良野町　Brilliance

朝の陰影・美瑛町　Morning's rhythmic patterns

午後の陰影・美瑛町　Afternoon shadows　*83*

霧氷の朝・上富良野町　Silver-frosted snowscape

ひとすじの道・上富良野町　Solitary Road

PHOTOGRAPHIC DATA

SPRING, SUMMER, AUTUMN AND WINTER

5——HASSELBLAD 500C/M TELE-TESSAR 500mm F8 f32 1/125
6——LINHOF SUPER TECHNIKA 4×5 NIKKOR 150mm F5.6 f32 1/4
7——HASSELBLAD 500C/M TELE-TESSAR 500mm F8 f32 1/4
8——LINHOF SUPER TECHNIKA 4×5 FUJINON 400mm F8 f22 1/15
9——LINHOF SUPER TECHNIKA 4×5 NIKKOR 150mm F5.6 f32 1/8
10——TOYO FIELD 8×10 FUJINON 300mm F5.6 f32 1/15
11——LINHOF SUPER TECHNIKA 4×5 FUJINON 400mm F8 f22 1/15
12——TOYO FIELD 8×10 NIKKOR 450mm F9 f45 1/2
13——LINHOF SUPER TECHNIKA 4×5 NIKKOR 210mm F5.6 f22 1/15
14——LINHOF SUPER TECHNIKA 4×5 NIKKOR 150mm F5.6 f32 1/8
15——LINHOF SUPER TECHNIKA 4×5 NIKKOR 150mm F5.6 f16 1/15
16——LINHOF SUPER TECHNIKA 4×5 FUJINON 400mm F8 f32 1/8
17——LINHOF SUPER TECHNIKA 4×5 FUJINON 400mm F8 f22 1/30
18——LINHOF SUPER TECHNIKA 4×5 FUJINON 400mm F8 f16 1/15
19——LINHOF SUPER TECHNIKA 4×5 FUJINON 400mm F8 f22 1/15
20·21——TOYO FIELD 8×10 FUJINON 300mm F5.6 f45 1/4
22——LINHOF SUPER TECHNIKA 4×5 SUPER-ANGULON 90mm F8 f22 1/8
23——LINHOF SUPER TECHNIKA 4×5 FUJINON 250mm F6.3 f22 1/8
24——TOYO FIELD 4×5 FUJINON 600mm F11 f45 1/4
25——LINHOF SUPER TECHNIKA 4×5 NIKKOR 150mm F5.6 f32 1/8
26·27——LINHOF SUPER TECHNIKA 4×5 FUJINON 400mm F8 f22 1/15
28——HASSELBLAD SWC BIOGON 38mm F4.5 f22 1/15
29——HASSELBLAD SWC BIOGON 38mm F4.5 f11 1/60 (F)
30——HASSELBLAD 500C/M DISTAGON 60mm F3.5 f16 1/30
31——LINHOF SUPER TECHNIKA 4×5 FUJINON 250mm F6.3 f22 1/15
32——LINHOF SUPER TECHNIKA 4×5 FUJINON 125mm F5.6 f22 1/15
33——HASSELBLAD SWC BIOGON 38mm F4.5 f11 1/60
34——LINHOF SUPER TECHNIKA 4×5 SUPER-ANGULON 90mm F8 f8 1sec.
35——HASSELBLAD SWC BIOGON 38mm F4.5 f16 1/15
36——LINHOF SUPER TECHNIKA 4×5 FUJINON 250mm F6.3 f22 1/15
37——LINHOF SUPER TECHNIKA 4×5 SUPER-ANGULON 90mm F8 f32 1/15
38——LINHOF SUPER TECHNIKA 4×5 SUPER-ANGULON 90mm F8 f22 1/60
39——LINHOF SUPER TECHNIKA 4×5 SUPER-ANGULON 90mm F8 f16 1/30
40——HASSELBLAD 500C/M SONNAR 250mm F5.6 f32 1/8
41——LINHOF SUPER TECHNIKA 4×5 FUJINON 400mm F8 f22 1/15
42·43——LINHOF SUPER TECHNIKA 4×5 SUPER-ANGULON 90mm F8 f22 1/30
44——HASSELBLAD 500C/M PLANAR 100mm F3.5 f16 1/4
45——HASSELBLAD SWC BIOGON 38mm F4.5 f22 1/30
46——HASSELBLAD 500C/M PLANAR 100mm F3.5 f22 1/60
47——LINHOF SUPER TECHNIKA 4×5 NIKKOR 150mm F5.6 f22 1/30
48——LINHOF SUPER TECHNIKA 4×5 SUPER-ANGULON 90mm F8 f16 1/30
49——LINHOF SUPER TECHNIKA 4×5 FUJINON 400mm F8 f32 1/8

50——LINHOF SUPER TECHNIKA 4×5 NIKKOR 210mm F5.6 f16 1/30
51——HASSELBLAD 500C/M SONNAR 250mm F5.6 f22 1/8
52——LINHOF SUPER TECHNIKA 4×5 NIKKOR 150mm F5.6 f32 1/4
53——LINHOF SUPER TECHNIKA 4×5 TELE-XENAR 360mm F5.5 f32 1/8
54——HASSELBLAD 500C/M SONNAR 250mm F5.6 f22 1/8
55——TOYO FIELD 4×5 FUJINON 600mm F11 f45 1/4
56——HASSELBLAD 500C/M SONNAR 250mm F5.6 f22 1/8
57——LINHOF SUPER TECHNIKA 4×5 FUJINON 400mm F8 f32 1/8
58——LINHOF SUPER TECHNIKA 4×5 FUJINON 400mm F8 f22 1/30
59——TOYO FIELD 4×5 FUJINON 600mm F11 f11 1/8
60——LINHOF SUPER TECHNIKA 4×5 FUJINON 250mm F6.3 f32 1/4
61——LINHOF SUPER TECHNIKA 4×5 FUJINON 400mm F8 f32 1/8
62——TOYO FIELD 4×5 FUJINON 600mm F11 f45 1/4
63——LINHOF SUPER TECHNIKA 4×5 FUJINON 400mm F8 f22 1/8
64——LINHOF SUPER TECHNIKA 4×5 TELE-XENAR 360mm F5.5 f5.5 1/60
65——TOYO FIELD 8×10 FUJINON 300mm F5.6 f32 1/4
66——HASSELBLAD 500C/M TELE-TESSAR 500mm F8 f32 1sec.
67——LINHOF SUPER TECHNIKA 4×5 FUJINON 400mm F8 f32 1/4
68——HASSELBLAD 500C/M SONNAR 250mm F5.6 f32 1/8
69——HASSELBLAD 500C/M PLANAR 100mm F3.5 f22 1/8
70——HASSELBLAD 500C/M SONNAR 250mm F5.6 f22 1/2
71——HASSELBLAD 500C/M SONNAR 250mm F5.6 f22 1/4
72——HASSELBLAD 500C/M SONNAR 250mm F5.6 f22 1/4
73——HASSELBLAD 500C/M SONNAR 250mm F5.6 f22 1/8
74——LINHOF SUPER TECHNIKA 4×5 SUPER-ANGULON 90mm F8 f22 1/30
75——LINHOF SUPER TECHNIKA 4×5 FUJINON 400mm F8 f32 1/30
76——HASSELBLAD 500C/M SONNAR 250mm F5.6 f32 1/2 (F)
77——LINHOF SUPER TECHNIKA 4×5 NIKKOR 210mm F5.6 f32 1/4
78——LINHOF SUPER TECHNIKA 4×5 SUPER-ANGULON 90mm F8 f32 1/60
79——LINHOF SUPER TECHNIKA 4×5 FUJINON 400mm F8 f32 1/30
80——HASSELBLAD 500C/M PLANAR 100mm F3.5 f32 1/4
81——HASSELBLAD 500C/M DISTAGON 60mm F3.5 f22 1/30
82——HASSELBLAD 500C/M SONNAR 250mm F5.6 f22 1/30
83——HASSELBLAD 500C/M SONNAR 250mm F5.6 f32 1/15
84——HASSELBLAD 500C/M PLANAR 100mm F3.5 f22 1/30
85——LINHOF SUPER TECHNIKA 4×5 TELE-XENAR 360mm F5.5 f22 1/15
86——LINHOF SUPER TECHNIKA 4×5 NIKKOR 150mm F5.6 f32 1/15
87——HASSELBLAD 500C/M TELE-TESSAR 500mm F8 f16 1/60
88——HASSELBLAD 500C/M PLANAR 100mm F3.5 f8 30sec.

FILM——表示のないものは，EKTACHROME(EPR ASA 64)を使用。
　　　　FUJICHROME (RFP ASA 50)を使用したものは，(F)と表示。

あとがき――――――――前田真三

旭川から国道237号線を富良野方面に30キロ程南下したあたりで、国道は小高い丘を越え、いくつかの峠にさしかかる。この付近、美瑛町、上富良野町の一帯には、日本離れのした丘が続いている。この丘に魅せられ、通い続けて既に15年になろうとしている。この丘を語るにはまず旭川の大谷全さんと美馬牛峠(P.88)に程近い津郷(P.32,85)で農業を営んでいる泉隆春さんのことを書いておかなければならない。

昭和46年(1971) 3月、自動車による単独での日本縦断撮影旅行を思い立ち、九州最南端の佐多岬を出発したのが4月1日であった。岬の灯台は、春の海にかすんでいた。その日から一路北上を続けて、三ヶ月後の7月8日にようやく北海道北端の宗谷岬に到達した。そして稚内から南下の途中、知人の紹介で知り合った旭川の大谷さんの家に立ち寄った。写真の好きな大谷さんは、大雪山や旭川付近をよく撮り歩いていて、その時私にたくさんの写真を見せてくれた。その中の一枚に、傾斜した畑を農耕馬が土煙を上げて驀進してくるモノクロームの写真があった。その写真自体も迫力があって良い写真だと思ったが、その背景になっている落葉松の丘が妙に心に残った。その場所は美馬牛峠付近とのことであったので、帰りに都合でちょっとのぞいて見ようと思った。大谷さんに別れを告げて、二、三日大雪山周辺で過ごした。そして美馬牛峠にさしかかったのが、忘れもしない昭和46年7月12日の昼下がりのことであった。次の文は、その時の模様を数年前出版した『北海道――大地の詩』と題する写真集に書いた一節である。

『爽やかな初夏の風が心地よく丘を吹き抜けていた。あたり一面真白いジャガイモの花畑である。
ゆるやかな丘は適当な起状を保ちながら果てしなく続いている。空は抜けるように青い。
目を東に向けると、眩しいばかりの残雪の中に噴煙を真直ぐ天に突きあげている十勝岳の主峰。
やや北に目を転ずると、トムラウシから大雪連峰が指呼の間に望まれる。
先程から私は余りにも大きく美しい眼前の風景に心を奪われていた。かつてこれだけおおらかで、
心にふれる風景に出会ったことがあったであろうか。……この丘との最初の出会いである。』

そしてこの日、はからずも、もうひとつの出会いがあった。泉隆春さんとの出会いである。丘に連なる落葉松林を撮影中、測量と間違えられて怒鳴られる一幕もあったが、写真を撮らせてもらっている旨説明すると、拍子抜けした様子で家に寄ってお茶でも飲んで行きなさいということになった。このことがきっかけとなって、以来泉さん一家との交流が始まり、次第にこの丘を訪ねる機会も多くなっていった。

泉さんは上富良野町の教育委員等もしていた関係で、私のことを理解し応援してくれたものであろう。泉さんとの出会いがなかったら、私もここまでこの丘に通いつめることが出来なかったろうし、またこの写真集も世に出る機会がなかったかもしれないと思っている。

その日の夕暮近く残照に映える十勝連峰を左手に見ながら私は、美馬牛峠から心も軽やかに開運坂(現在はこの名称は使われていない)を越えて行った。今にして思えば、その名の如く正に開運坂であった。

最近では、この地を訪れる観光客も随分多くなった。その目的のひとつにラベンダーがある。今から十数年前は、北海道各地でラベンダーを見ることができた。特にこの地方では、7月下旬になるとあちらの丘にもこちらの丘にも、紫色のラベンダー畑が目についたものである。南ヨーロッパ原産のこの花は、西洋風のこの丘陵地帯にまことによく似合った花である。残念ながらその後減少の一途をたどってこの付近でもほとんどなくなってしまった(P.29, 38)。最近では地元の上富良野町などでも栽培に力をいれているので(P.40)、次第に復活の兆しが見えてきたことは喜ばしいことである。そうした中にあって、中富良野町の富田忠雄氏のように孤塁よく今日までラベンダーを守ってきた人もいる(P.33)。

ラベンダーに限らず、この付近で栽培されている作物も、年と共に多少変化しているようである。主流はジャガイモ(P.32)、ビート、小麦(P.24, 25, 26～27, 30, 31, 36, 39, 57, 62)、小豆などの豆類(P.48, 49, 54)や疏菜などであるが、最近玉葱(P.55)なども多く見られるようになった。また近頃は、ポピー等の花(P.28)もいくらか作られ、彩り豊かな丘に一層花を添えている。これらの作物が春から夏、夏から秋の収穫へと豊かな色や形で丘を彩って行く。この丘の最も大きな魅力のひとつである。もうひとつの忘れてはならないのが大雪、十勝、芦別などの山々である。これらの連峰が単調になりがちな丘の景観を引きしめている。そして更にこれら丘の主役達を引き立てる役割を果たしているのが、丘のあちこちに点在する落葉松や白樺、ポプラなどの木々である。あるものは畑の中に一本、またあるものは丘の頂きに整然と並んで、この丘陵地帯の景観に一役買っている。

この写真集に収録されている写真は、過去十数年間に撮影したフィルムの中から選出して、丘の美しい表情を正面に打ち出して編集したものである。丘のおおらかで、広がりのある雰囲気を出したいと思ったので、花や木、作物などのアップの写真は極力割愛した。そして人工的な畑作地帯とはいえ、この丘もまた自然の摂理に支配されている。いつでもこの様に美しい表情ばかりではなく、その裏に隠されている厳しい面も合わせて理解していただければと思う。

尚、この写真集の中には、既に切られてなくなってしまった落葉松など(P.7, 9, 14, 26～27, 42～43, 57, 74, 78, 85)、道路拡張や耕地整理などの為に地形が変わってしまったり(P.10, 37, 49, 50, 65, 83)、あるいは台風などで倒れたり、傾いてしまった並木や畑の中の木(P.11, 25)など、二度と撮ることのできない写真もたくさん含まれている。「風景を出会いの瞬間に捉えること」は、常に変わらぬ私の身上であるが、風景写真はその時々を大切に撮りたいと改めて思う。

この写真集では個々の写真に対して、細かい解説をしていないが、私が感じてシャッターを切った様に、それぞれの立場で、それぞれの写真を見ていただければ幸いである。

最後に、永い間御世話になった泉さん一家をはじめ大谷さんほかたくさんの方々に深く感謝の意を表し、厚く御礼申し上げる次第である。

Afterword

Shinzo Maeda

The national highway from Asahikawa to Furano runs through numerous small hills before it finally reches the area's mountain passes, and in the vicinity of the towns of Biei and Kamifurano one can see hills of a distinctly non-Japanese type. Though it has been almost fifteen years since my first visit to that district, I am still deeply moved each time I gaze upon those hills. But before I say anything more about the hills, I must mention my first meetings with two men who greatly assisted me during my rambles through the Hokkaido hills. One was Mr. Akira Otani of Asahikawa and the other Mr. Takaharu Izumi, a farmer from Tsugo (p. 32, 85). In 1971 I set out upon a long photographic journey;my goal was to drive the length of Japan, taking pictures all the way. I started out from Sata Point at the southernmost tip of the island of Kyushu, and I departed on the first day of April, looking back only briefly for one last glimpse of the dimly outlined lighthouse on the promontory overlooking the spring sea. A little over three months later, I at last arrived at Soya Point on the north end of the island of Hokkaido. Heading south on my way back, I stopped at the Asahikawa home of the aforementioned Mr. Otani, to whom I had been given an introduction. Mr. Otani, a camera enthusiast, often went hiking and picture taking, and he had many photographs that he had taken around Mt. Daisetsu and the Asahikawa area. Among those that he showed me was one monochrome of a farmer's horse racing down a hillside, trailing a cloud of dust. The photograph itself was powerful and greatly impressed me, but somehow the hilltop larches in the background were what most firmly held my eye. When I mentioned that fact, my host told me that they were near Bibaushi Pass, so I decided to stop there and see the place.

After leaving Mr. Otani's home, I spent a few days around Mt. Daisetsu and then headed directly for Bibaushi Pass. I will never forget that early afternoon on July 12, 1971. Perhaps I can best explain how I felt by quoting a passage from one of my earlier books "Hokkaido—Poetry of the Earth."

> A refreshing early summer breeze moved across rolling fields blanketed with white potato blossoms;the hills gently rose and fell as they endlessly stretched toward the horizon. Above, the sky was as blue as blue could ever be. I looked eastward and saw the volcanic smoke curl from Mt.Tokachi and soar high above the dazzlingly white snow which still remained on the ground. Enthralled by the spectacle, I stood and gazed at the beauty before me, asking myself, "Have I ever before come across scenery so dynamic ———and yet so touching?"

Such were my feelings.

On that same July day, I had an unexpected and interesting encounter which began my acquaintance with Mr. Takaharu Izumi, a local farmer, and the other person who greatly assisted me in my work. While I was photographing a larch forest near some hills, Mr. Izumi, perhaps thinking I was a nosey surveyor or something, came over to shoo me away. When I explained that I was merely taking pictures, he seemed at a loss what to say, so he did the friendly thing and invited me to his home for a cup of tea. That cup of tea was the start of my friendship with the Izumis and led to many future visits to the hills near their home.

Mr. Izumi, who was a member of the local board of education at the time, was helpful and understanding in countless ways. Had I not met and come to know him, it is unlikely that I would have centered my work on the hills, and the photographs in this book might never have been taken.

I recall that on the evening of the day I met Mr. Izumi, I took a pleasant stroll down one of the hills leading from Bibaushi Pass. To my left, the Tokachi Mountains glowed in the evening sky, enhancing the beauty and serenity around me. The hill I walked upon was named Kaiunzaka, which means Hill of Good Fortune, and now when I think about it, I have the feeling that the hill was quite aptly named, at least for me.

In recent years, the number of sightseers coming to the hill district has greatly increased, and one of the reasons for this is the lovely lavender fields that may be found there. Ten or fifteen years ago, lavender was scattered throughout Hokkaido, and those fields of purple added a special touch of beauty, perhaps in part because the lavender is a native of Europe and so goes well with the western-looking hills of the area. I am sorry to say, however, that many hills of lavender have disappeared and now there are few to be seen even in the Asahikawa-Furano region (p. 29, 38). But in recent years, the people of Kamifurano Town have worked hard to raise more lavender, and it is heartening to see the lavender fields are gradually making a comeback (p. 40). Mr. Tadao Tomita, whose farm is shown in this book (p. 33) is one local farmer whose life has been closely tied to the lovely blossoms, and he has always grown lavender regardless of the changes that have taken place in the land around him.

The lavender fields have not been the only things which have felt the pressures of change. Traditionally the main crops of the hill district have mostly been vegetables——potatoes (p. 32), beets, wheat (p. 24, 25, 26~27, 30, 31, 36, 39, 57, 62) and various beans (p. 48, 49, 54). But there has been a marked increase in the acreage devoted to onions (p. 55) and recently farmers have begun to raise poppies (p. 28), a happy move which has further brightened the already colorful hills.

I have been talking about the hills and crops of the district, but I should not overlook the surrounding mountains——Mt. Daisetsu, Mt. Tokachi, Mt. Ashibetsu and others. The local peaks put accents on the more subdued scenery in the hill district. And the trees——larches, white birches, poplars and the like——make their contributions as supporting actors in the natural drama that unfolds for the visitor. Some stand alone on the fields, others in neat rows along the slopes of the hills. All help to create a special hill country atmosphere.

The photographs collected in this book are those I have taken over the last fifteen or sixteen years. I have edited them so as to bring to the forefront the beautiful expressions of the hills, and in order to emphasize a panoramic view, I have subordinated closeups of trees, flowers and farm crops as much as possible. I hope that those looking at this will understand that the hills do not always possess the kind of beauty displayed in these photos ; even man-made farmland is subject to the influences of the forces of nature, and the hills are capable of putting forth other and more severe countenances.

I should also add that this collection includes many photographs which can never be retaken, because what they show no longer exists. In place the landscape has changed because of roadbuilding or adjustments of arable land (p. 10, 37, 49, 50, 65, 83). Some of the larches shown here have been cut down (p. 7, 9, 14, 26~27, 42~43, 57, 74, 78, 85) and other trees have been blown down or damaged by typhoons (p. 11, 25).

"To catch scenery at the moment of encounter" has always been my principle, and I must remember that every single picture I take is the capturing of a precious moment. In this book, I have avoided making individual comments on each photograph, hoping instead that as you look at the pictures you will judge and appreciate them in your own very personal way, just as I did when I released the shutter on my camera.

In conclusion, I would like to express my sincere gratitude to Mr. Takaharu Izumi and his family, who supported me for so long, and to Mr. Akira Otani and the many other people who helped bring this work to completion.

前田真三略歴・BIOGRAPHY——SHINZO MAEDA

1922	東京都八王子市下恩方町に生まれる
1948	ニチメン(株)に入社、以後17年間勤務
1967	フォト・エージェンシー(株)丹渓を設立、代表となる。同時に写真活動に入る
1968	日本の風景に的を絞って本格的に写真を撮り始め、出版・広告・デザイン関係に写真提供を開始する
1971	企業のカレンダー・PR誌・ポスター等多くの媒体に写真を提供、新しい形の風景写真家としての基盤を築く
1973	毎日新聞社『日本の四季』を始めとする「四季シリーズ」及び様々な出版物に写真を寄稿
1974	写真集『ふるさとの四季』(毎日新聞社)
1976	写真集『日本の彩』(旅行読売出版社)
	写真集『ふるさとの山河』(毎日新聞社)
1977	写真集『出合の瞬間』(毎日新聞社)
	全国カレンダー展で大蔵省印刷局長賞(丹渓)受賞
1978	写真集『春夏秋冬』(国際情報社)
	フォトキナ(西ドイツ・ケルン)に日本代表として出展
1979	朝日広告賞(麒麟麦酒の新聞広告)受賞
1980	ユーロ・フォト(スペイン・マジョルカ島)に日本代表として出展
	全国カレンダー展で内閣総理大臣賞(積水ハウス)、大蔵省印刷局長賞(ホクレン)受賞
1981	写真集『北海道——大地の詩』(集英社)
	全国カレンダー展で日本印刷工業会会長賞(シュリロ・トレーディング)受賞
1982	写真集『山河有情』(保育社)
	全国カレンダー展で印刷時報社賞(ホクレン、丹渓)受賞
	国際カレンダー展(西ドイツ)で優秀カレンダー賞銀賞(丹渓)受賞
1983	写真集『一木一草』(グラフィック社)
	写真集『昭和写真全仕事・前田真三』(朝日新聞社)
	全国カレンダー展で日本印刷工業会会長賞(丹渓)受賞
	国際カレンダー展(西ドイツ)で最優秀カレンダー賞金賞・最優秀写真賞(丹渓)受賞
1984	写真集『上高地』(グラフィック社)
	写真集『ランドスケープ・フォトグラフィー(世界の風景写真家8人集)』(アメリカ・アムフォト)
	写真展(西ドイツ・ハンブルグ 9月、フランス・パリ '85年2月)
	日本写真協会年度賞を受賞
1985	写真集『奥三河』(グラフィック社)
	写真集『四季百景』(日本カメラ社)
	写真集『山野逍遙』(毎日新聞社)
	第39回毎日出版文化賞特別賞を受賞(『奥三河』)
	日本国内では写真展を20数回開催
	日本写真家協会・自然科学写真協会・日本山岳写真協会会員

Office 前田真三写真事務所 株式会社 丹渓
〒107 東京都港区北青山2-7-26 メゾン青山402 電話03-405-1681

1922	Born in Shimo-Ongata-cho, Hachioji City, Tokyo
1948	Employed by Nichimen Co., Ltd., works there for the net 17 years
1967	Founds Tankei Photo Agency Co., Ltd., becomes a professional photographer
1968	Focuses work on photographs of Japanese scenery, devoting full time to photography. Begins offering work to publishers, advertisers and design companies
1971	Lays groundwork for new type of scenic photography, offering photos to many media for commercial calendars, PR magazines and commercial posters
1973	Contributes many photos in publications such as "The Four Seasons in Japan" and other books in the "Four Seasons" series published by the Mainichi Newspapers.
1974	Publishes "The Four Seasons of a Home Town" (The Mainichi Newspapers)
1976	Publishes "The Colors of Japan" (Ryoko Yomiuri Publishing Co.)
	Publishes "The Mountains and Rivers of a Home Town" (The Mainichi Newspapers)
1977	Publishes "The Moment of Encounter" (The Mainichi Newspapers)
	Receives Finance Ministry Printing Bureau Director's Award at All Japan Calendar Fair
1978	Publishes "Spring, Summer, Autumn and Winter" (Kokusai Johosha Publishing Co.)
	Exhibits at Fotokina (Köln, West Germany) as representative of Japan.
1979	Receives Asahi Advertising prize
1980	Exhibits at Europhoto (Majorca, Spain) as representative of Japan
	Receives Prime Minister's Award and Finance Ministry Printing Bureau Director's Award at All Japan Calecdar Fair
1981	Publishes "Hokkaido-Poetry of the Earth" (Shueisha Publishing Co.)
	Receives Japan Printing Industry President's Award at All Japan Calendar Fair
1982	Publishes "Scenes From Nature" (Hoikusha Publishing Co.)
	Receives Insatsu-Jiho-sha Co. Award at All Japan Calendar Fair
	Receives Silver Award for Excellence at International Calendar Fair. (West Germany)
1983	Publishes "A Tree, A Blade of Grass" (Graphic-sha Publishing Co.).
	Publishes "Shinzo Maeda" (Asahi Shimbun)
	Receives Japan Printing Industry President's Award at All Japan Calendar Fair
	Receives Golden Award for Most Excellent Calendar and Most Excellent Photography Award at International Calendar Fair. (West Germany)
1984	Publishes "The Nippon Alps, Kamikochi" (Graphic-sha Publishing Co.)
	Contributes in the book "Landscape Photography" (Amphoto, U.S.A.)
	Holds the Exhibition "A Tree, A Blade of Grass" (Hamburg, West Germany September, Paris, France February 1985)
	Receives Annual Award of the Photographic Society of Japan
1985	Publishes "Okumikawa" (Graphic-sha Publishing Co.)
	Publishes "Scenes in Four Seasons" (Nippon Camera Publishing Co.)
	Publishes "Ambling in Nature" (The Mainichi Newspapers)
	Receives Special Award at the Thirty-ninth Mainichi Publications Culture Competition for the book "Okumikawa"
	Shinzo Maeda has helds more than twenty-five photo exhibitions in Japan
	Member of Japan Professional Photograpers Society, Society of Scientific Photograph, Japan Alpine Photographers Association

Office Shinzo Maeda Photography Office, Tankei Co., Ltd.
402 Maison Aoyama, 2-7-26 Kita-Aoyama, Minato-ku, Tokyo Japan 107
Phone. 03-405-1681

晩秋の丘にて　1985年10月　On a hill in late autumn, October 1985

付録写真：大雪山幻想・美瑛町　Evening fantasy——Mt. Daisetsu

丘の四季

撮影 前田真三

HILLS OF COLOR Scenes and Seasons

Photographed by Shinzo Maeda

1986年 4月25日　　初版第一刷発行

定価 3,800円　乱丁・落丁はお取替えいたします。

発 行 者　久世利郎

発 行 所　株式会社グラフィック社

〒102 東京都千代田区九段北1-9-12

PHONE 03-263-4318

印　刷　凸版印刷株式会社

製　本　凸版製本株式会社

写　植　三和写真工芸㈱